EASY JUICING

EASY JUICING

THE BEST 100 JUICES, CRUSHES, SMOOTHIES, COOLERS AND QUENCHERS

NICOLA GRAIMES

DUNCAN BAIRD PUBLISHERS

LONDON

Easy Juicing
Nicola Graimes

First published in the United Kingdom and Ireland in 2006 by
Duncan Baird Publishers Ltd
Sixth Floor, Castle House
75–76 Wells Street, London W1T 3QH

Created and designed by Duncan Baird Publishers

Associate Author: Julia Charles
Managing Editor: Grace Cheetham
Editor: Ingrid Court-Jones
Managing Designer: Daniel Sturges
Designer: Gail Jones
Commissioned artwork: Karine Faou@eyecandy

Library of Congress Cataloging-in-Publication Data is available

Distributed in the United States and Canada by
Sterling Publishing Co., Inc.
387 Park Avenue South,
New York, NY 10016-8810

ISBN-13: 9-781844-833122   ISBN-10: 1-84483-312-7

10 9 8 7 6 5 4 3 2

Typeset in Champion and Clarendon
Color reproduction by Colourscan, Singapore
Printed in China by Imago

Publishers' Notes
All recipes serve 2, unless otherwise stated. Some of the recipes in this book contain raw eggs and peanut
products, which may be unsuitable for some people. If you are in any doubt as to the suitability of any of the
recipes given herein, consult your doctor. The Publishers and the Author cannot accept any responsibility for
any problems that arise as a result of preparing any of the recipes given in this book.

To Silvio, Joel and Ella

[CONTENTS]

[03] COOLERS AND QUENCHERS 054

[REFRESHING ice-blended juices for hot summer days]

[04] PICK-ME-UPS AND REVIVERS 076

[particularly potent blends to NOURISH body and mind]

[05] TIPPLES 098

[juices, smoothies, coolers and quenchers with a dash of alcohol for SPECIAL occasions]

LET'S GET JUICING

Nothing beats a fresh fruit juice – from the simplicity of a tangy "OJ" (orange juice) to the velvety decadence of a mango smoothie. Of course, you can buy ready-made drinks, but it's much more fun to turn your own kitchen into a juice bar and enjoy the pleasures of made-to-order fresh juice every day.

Not only is juicing at home a treat for your taste buds and kinder on your purse, but it's also very good for you. The nutrients in freshly-made fruit juices are big health-boosters and can do a whole bunch of good things, such as improve the condition of your skin, help you to detox, protect you from colds and flu, boost your energy levels and enhance your vitality.

In this book you'll find 100 fantastic recipes for everything from delicious juices and crushes to luxurious smoothies and blends; refreshing coolers and quenchers to health-boosting pick-me-ups and revivers and, as an extra special treat, some naughty but nice alcoholic tipples.

To get started you'll need some equipment. For juices that include citrus fruit, you can use a hand-held wooden citrus juicer or "reamer". You'll also need a juicer. It's not necessary to buy an expensive model immediately, but if you think you are going to become a juice junkie, it's worth investing in a high-powered one with a strong motor. For making smoothies, cocktails and milkshakes, you'll require a blender. Look for a model that has various speeds and functions so that you can use it for chopping and puréeing, as well as crushing ice or blending frozen fruit. Check that your equipment is easy to dismantle and clean, and always wash or rinse it straight after use. Time spent scrubbing off dried-on fruit pulp is not time well spent!

You don't always need to remove the skin from fruit and veg before juicing or blending, but always wash or scrub it thoroughly. Most of the nutrients are found in or just below the skin, so it's best to leave produce intact wherever possible. However, any fruit or veg with thick skin, such as melons, pineapples and squashes, are too tough for even the most powerful machines, so you'll need to peel them and cut the flesh into smallish chunks. When juicing herbs or salad leaves, roll them into a bundle or wrap them around another vegetable for maximum juice extraction. Always drink your juices soon after you've made them, as they soon oxidize and lose nutrient content, colour and taste.

For the scrummiest drinks buy organic produce, because it's usually more nutritious and you'll avoid nasty chemical pesticides and fertilizers. For maximum flavour and biggest juice yield, it's best to use fruit that's just ripe. Don't be tempted to use battered, blemished or mouldy produce – it just won't taste or look nice. Always choose good-quality, fresh ingredients and you won't go far wrong.

Pure, clean fruit and vegetable juices feed, replenish and invigorate your mind, body and spirit throughout the day. So come on – plug in your juicer or blender, choose your fruit or veg and say hello to the wonderful world of juicing – the twenty-first-century way to nourish yourself.

Delicious, fresh, healthy and energising ... enjoying a freshly-pressed fruit juice every day can be a truly life-enhancing activity – in more ways than one!

JUICES AND CRUSHES

Did you know that by making your own fresh juices you will be going that extra mile and ensuring that the nutrients in every mouthful you savour are being delivered to your body super-fast? Fantastic isn't it? But let's not forget that they are also delicious, and drinking a mouth-watering juice brings enormous pleasure. Here are some quick and simple recipes for juices and crushes that knock the socks off anything you can buy in cartons or bottles. So ... what are you waiting for? Let's get juicing!

2 large green tart APPLES (such as
Granny Smith), stalks removed,
and quartered
2 medium-sized CARROTS, chopped
2.5cm/1in piece fresh GINGER ROOT, peeled
freshly-squeezed LEMON juice, to taste
long floppy ears (optional)

[001]

BUGS BUNNY

This tangy and invigorating blend of fruit
and veggies is simplicity itself to make and
absolutely guaranteed to have you bouncing
around like a bunny! What gives this juice
its extra zing is the addition of deliciously
spicy fresh ginger. Simply juice the prepared
apples and carrots with the ginger, pour
into two tall, freezer-frosted glasses
and stir in a good squeeze of fresh
lemon juice just before serving.

[002]

SUN
SALUTE

This drink makes an ultra-refreshing start
to the day. Choose firm fruits that feel heavy
for their size, as this means they will be
juicy. Use a citrus press or reamer to juice
the oranges and the grapefruit. Add the
lemon juice, stir and serve. For a longer
drink, pour into a highball glass filled with
crushed ice, top up with a squirt of soda or
sparkling mineral water and you have the
perfect post-yoga-workout refresher.

2 ORANGES, halved
1 pink GRAPEFRUIT, halved
1 tbsp freshly-squeezed LEMON juice

Try putting your chopped basil in an ice-cube tray, topping it up with water and freezing it. Crush the basil ice and spoon it into shot glasses, pour in the juice and drizzle balsamic vinegar into each one before serving.

12 vine-ripened TOMATOES, halved
1 stick CELERY
1 mild red CHILLI, deseeded
1/4 tsp balsamic VINEGAR
freshly-squeezed juice of 1/4 LEMON
2 large BASIL leaves, finely chopped
freshly ground black PEPPER

[003]
SPICY ITALIAN

It's time to come over all Italian and give those tomatoes a squeeze before you buy them, because the secret of this juice lies in the quality of its ingredients. The chilli adds spice in more ways than one as it's thought to be an aphrodisiac! Juice the tomatoes, celery and chilli. Add the vinegar, lemon juice, basil and pepper, and pour into two glasses.

[004]
RISE N' SHINE

Reach for your sunglasses – this combo makes a
day-glo orange juice guaranteed to bring a ray of
sunshine to the gloomiest of mornings. Pineapples
are packed with vitamins and minerals so they
make a perfect addition to this traditional
breakfast blend. First, juice the pineapple. Then,
use a citrus press or reamer to squeeze the juice
from the oranges and the grapefruit. Combine the
pineapple and citrus juices and pour
into two glasses to serve.

$1/2$ medium PINEAPPLE, peeled and chopped
2 ORANGES, halved
1 pink GRAPEFRUIT, halved
a pair of shades (optional)

[005]
PURE
NECTAR

Beware of the bees! Make sure that your windows are shut because this thick, sticky juice is a heady blend of pure goodness. For best results, choose nectarines that are tender when you squeeze them gently in your hand. Put the nectarines and clementines through a juicer, then pour into glasses and add ice before serving. Tastes too good to be true!

6 NECTARINES, stoned and chopped
3 CLEMENTINES, peeled
ICE, to serve

JUST [006] PEACHY

One sip of this succulent blend and you will be transported to a sunlight-dappled orchard full of trees heavy with ripe, fragrant fruits … . It's best to use slightly under-ripe pears as they give you a thicker juice with more bite. Just juice the prepared fruit before adding a squeeze of lemon juice to taste. Serve in tall glasses filled with crushed ice.

2 PEARS, stalks removed, and quartered
4 APRICOTS, stoned and chopped
3 PEACHES, stoned and chopped
freshly-squeezed LEMON juice, to taste
a free afternoon (optional)

1 medium PINEAPPLE, peeled and chopped
1/2 Cantaloupe MELON, peeled,
deseeded and cut into wedges

[007] SUMO

Take pineapple and melon – two heavyweights
of the fruit world – and let them fight it out in
a big, fat juice packed with flavour. Because
melons have a high water content, they can
help to eliminate excess fluid from the body,
making this a very useful juice for when you
want to look your best in a slinky evening
dress. Just put all the fruit through
a juicer, stir and pour into glasses.

THANKS [008] A BUNCH

300g/10$\frac{1}{2}$oz white seedless GRAPES
3 green APPLES, stalks removed, and quartered
1 GRAPEFRUIT, halved

Be grateful to this unassuming yet delicious pale green juice. What for, you ask? Well, one sip and you'll know ... . As well as being deliciously sweet and refreshing, grapes are also highly nutritious and, unlike its fermented friend, this grape juice won't give you a headache if you over-indulge. Juice the grapes and the apples. Use a citrus press or reamer to juice the grapefruit. Mix everything together and serve.

[009]
SIDE DISH

This veggie and fruit combo shouldn't work but it does, and it makes a tasty, super-nutritious juice packed with vitamins and minerals. Undiluted veggie juices, with the exception of carrot, are challenging on the taste buds but they are good for you, so it's useful to know that by blending them with fruit you can enjoy both the benefits and the taste. Juice all the prepared ingredients and stir in the lemon juice before serving in tumblers.

2 APPLES, stalks removed, and quartered
1/4 medium red CABBAGE, outer leaves removed, and sliced
2 small SWEET POTATOES, cut into wedges
1 orange PEPPER, deseeded and sliced
freshly-squeezed LEMON juice, to taste

To make a sorbet, add a beaten egg white to the juice, pour into a container and freeze for 2 hours. Take it out, give it a good stir to break down the ice crystals and return to the freezer. Repeat this process twice before serving.

[010] IN
THE PINK

Teeny-weeny blackcurrants are the big boys when it comes to vitamin C and a glassful of this will soon put a rosy glow back into the palest cheeks. They have a satisfyingly tart flavour without being sour and will add a strong flavour to any juice. Fresh berries give the best results but you can use frozen or canned ones out of season. Juice all of the fruit together and serve. It's too easy, isn't it?

200g/7oz BLACKCURRANTS
2 APPLES, stalks removed, and quartered
2 PEARS, stalks removed, and quartered

1 MANGO, peeled and sliced
150g/5$1/2$ oz fresh RASPBERRIES
2 ORANGES, halved
crushed ICE, to serve
pigtails (optional)

[011]

SHERBET
DIB-DAB

This juice has a taste reminiscent of fruit sherbet
sweets. Go on, rediscover your inner child – skip if you
must! This also makes a refreshing long drink when
served in a tall glass with crushed ice and topped up
with sparkling water. Juice the mango and raspberries,
then use a citrus press or reamer to juice the oranges.
Combine everything, pour the juice into ice-filled
glasses, and add a pair of candy-striped straws to
each glass before serving.

[012]
KIWI PEEWEE

The kiwi is a hairy little fruit with a dull exterior that belies its surprisingly sweet green flesh. It's usually only seen in fruit salads, but mixed here with just a hint of lime juice it reveals itself to be not only small, but perfectly formed for juicing. To make this blend, simply juice the melon and the kiwi fruits together and add a squeeze of lime juice. Serve in tumblers full of crushed ice.

$1/2$ honeydew MELON, peeled deseeded and cut into wedges
2 KIWI FRUITS, peeled and quartered
freshly-squeezed juice of $1/2$ LIME

250g/9oz fresh BLACKBERRIES, hulled
8 purple PLUMS, stoned and chopped
ICE, to serve

[013] DEEP
PURPLE

Fancy a dramatic juice that really rocks? Then this
is the one for you. Its dark and moody appearance
masks a surprisingly fresh and fruity taste. If the
plums you use are a little tart and the resulting juice
has too much tang for your taste, simply add a little
sugar (you big softy, you). Juice the blackberries
followed by the plums. Pour into
glasses and serve with ice.

[014]

CAFÉ CULTURE

This is a highly sophisticated juice. The fennel gives it an aniseed flavour reminiscent of Pernod, the classic French aperitif, and its shocking pink colour makes it nothing short of avant garde! Put the prepared vegetables through the juicer. Use a citrus press or reamer to squeeze the juice from the oranges. Mix all the juices together and serve in tumblers.

1 medium FENNEL bulb, cut into long wedges
2 medium raw BEETROOTS, trimmed and cut into chunks
4 ORANGES, halved

[015]
MARILYN MANGO

Mango is the most delicious and luxurious of all tropical fruits and its meltingly soft flesh takes on an exquisite, velvety texture when it's blended. Use the tanginess of grapefruit to offset this sweetness and you'll have a voluptuous, full-bodied glassful with star quality. First, use a citrus press or reamer to squeeze all the juice from the grapefruit, then whizz the mango flesh in the blender. Simply mix the two juices together and pour into two glasses to serve.

1 pink GRAPEFRUIT, halved
1 large MANGO, peeled and sliced

This juice is great to have after you've eaten spicy food, such as Thai. For an extra kick, add a measure of cucumber vodka, and serve it in short tumblers, poured over crushed ice and garnished with a sprig of parsley. Perfect.

[016]

SPRING
CLEAN

This is a juice that will put the spring back in your step. As well as dusting off your taste buds, it will give you a good scrub and polish inside, as apples are nature's cleansers and detoxifiers. Juice the prepared apples and cucumber with one of the celery sticks. Pour into two ice-filled tumblers and garnish each glass with half the remaining stick of celery.

3 APPLES, stalks removed, and quartered
1 medium CUCUMBER, cut into long wedges
2 sticks CELERY
ICE, to serve

[017]

CLUB
TROPICANA

1/2 medium PAPAYA, peeled, deseeded
and chopped
1 medium MANGO, peeled and sliced
1/2 medium PINEAPPLE, peeled
and chopped
ICE, to serve

So what if you can't afford a luxury beach holiday this year. Turn up your central heating and take that well-earned break – even if it's only for the time it takes you to enjoy this golden-yellow and most tropical of juices! Whizz the prepared fruit in the juicer, pour into tall, ice-filled glasses and add straws and cocktail umbrellas. Drink while lying on a sun lounger (who cares if it's in your sitting room).

[018]

SWEETIE

You'll never to be mean to anyone ever again
once you've tasted this drink. How could you
be, in a world where such a darling juice
exists just to give you pleasure? The key
ingredient here is papaya – with its salmon-
pink flesh and a flavour that's a cross
between melon and peaches, it's the
perfect partner for strawberries. Juice
the fruits and pour into two glasses
to serve. What could be nicer?

1/2 medium PAPAYA, peeled,
deseeded and chopped
4 CLEMENTINES, peeled
300g/10 1/2 oz STRAWBERRIES,
hulled
freckles (optional)

BLOSSOM
[019]

This exotic juice is so pretty and fragrant that it
could well have been made from flower petals. Fresh
guavas are not widely available, but it's worth the
effort of trying to find them as they make a delicious
drink. Unsweetened guava nectar is more readily
available and you can substitute it here if necessary.
Juice the fruit and press it through a sieve to
make a smooth drink without any pips.
Pour into two glasses and serve.

**300g/10 1/2 oz fresh STRAWBERRIES, hulled
3 medium GUAVAS, peeled, deseeded and
quartered**

200g/7oz canned LYCHEES (drained weight)
8 MANDARINS, peeled
$1/2$ tsp ROSEWATER, or more to taste
ICE, to serve
a kimono (optional)

[020]
DRESS
TO IMPRESS

A taste of the Orient – juicy mandarins mingle with highly perfumed lychees to create a sublime juice fit for an Empress! Lychees have pearly flesh that is juicy and fragrant. In this blend the mandarins add a tang and the rosewater adds a delicate finishing touch. Juice the mandarins and lychees, then stir in the rosewater to taste. Serve with ice.

**Thick, creamy, velvety and satisfying ...
these drinks have a little more body
than just juice, so they'll not only fill
you up, but also keep you going.**

[SMOOTHIES AND BLENDS]

Now that you've got juicing under your belt, let's take
things one step further and venture into the heavenly
realm of smoothies and blends. Made by whizzing
virtually whole fruits together and adding yoghurt,
milk, soya milk, ice cream or sorbet, these treats are
definitely naughty – but still nice. How so? Because
they remain choc-a-block with all the nutrients found
in fruit, and the addition of dairy means that they
come with a built-in calcium boost. On top of this they
often include health-enhancing extras, such as wheat
germ. It just doesn't get any better than this!

1 MANGO, peeled and sliced
100ml/3^1/$_2$ fl oz WATER
120ml/8 tbsp natural BIO-YOGHURT
1–2 tsp caster SUGAR
300ml/^{1}/$_2$ pint semi-skimmed MILK
freshly-squeezed LIME juice, to taste

[021]
MONSOON

Who cares if there's a tropical rainstorm outside?
It's a good excuse to curl up indoors with a big
glassful of this creamy mango concoction.
Inspired by lassi, an Indian chilled buttermilk
drink, this is not as thick as your usual
smoothie and, as a result, it is more
refreshing. Whizz all the ingredients
(except the lime juice) in a blender until
light and frothy. Add a little squeeze
of lime juice to taste. Serve in long
glasses with ice.

[022]

BREAKFAST
FRAPPÉ

2 BANANAS, peeled and cut into chunks
200ml/7fl oz espresso COFFEE, cold
3 scoops real dairy VANILLA ICE CREAM
100ml/3$_{1/2}$ fl oz semi-skimmed MILK
6 ICE cubes, crushed
an early meeting (optional)

Here's something worth setting your alarm for! Bananas are the perfect ingredient for smoothies. Packed with fibre, vitamins and minerals, they turn any drink into a meal in a glass. They are also high in natural sugar, which provides a rapid energy boost and makes them a perfect breakfast food. What a good idea, then, to add a shot of coffee for that extra buzz! Simply blend the bananas with the coffee, ice cream, milk and crushed ice until thick and creamy, and serve.

2 BANANAS, peeled and cut into chunks
1 MANGO, peeled and sliced
200ml/7fl oz COCONUT MILK
200ml/7fl oz natural BIO-YOGHURT
seeds from 4 CARDAMOM PODS, crushed
with a pestle and mortar

[023]

MAHARAJAH

Fit for a maharajah, this decadent and indulgent smoothie has a magic ingredient – cardamom. With its rich aroma and warm, lemon- and eucalyptus-like flavours, cardamom is a key constituent in Indian spice mixes. It is also often used in drinks, in particular the spiced tea known as chai. Put both fruits in a blender and add the coconut milk and yoghurt. Whizz until frothy and smooth. Stir in the cardamom and serve in tall, ice-filled glasses.

For a real treat, add some broken meringue and a scoop of strawberry or vanilla ice cream. Pour into sundae glasses and serve with a spoon and a couple of straws. Heaven.

[024]
STRAWBERRY
SUNSHINE

Strawberries drizzled with fresh cream – a taste reminiscent of picnics on sunny summer days. And here it is again, only this time in a glass and made with no-less-creamy but reassuringly lower-in-fat Greek yoghurt that's been flavoured with luxurious real vanilla. Scrape the vanilla seeds into your blender. Add the rest of the ingredients and blend until smooth and creamy. Serve in two tall glasses.

1/2 VANILLA BEAN, split
350g/12oz STRAWBERRIES, hulled
150ml/5fl oz thick GREEK or Greek-style YOGHURT
350ml/12fl oz semi-skimmed MILK

[025]
SPECKLEBERRY

300g/10^1/$_2$ oz STRAWBERRIES, hulled
100g/3^1/$_2$ oz BLUEBERRIES
300ml/10fl oz freshly-squeezed ORANGE juice

This juice provides a major dose of vitamin C, as strawberries, blueberries and oranges all have it in abundance. Blueberries may be small, but what they lack in size they more than make up for in flavour. And they get top-billing here, as they give this juice its little blue specks, and thus, its name. Blend the two berries together. Mix in the orange juice until everything is well combined. Serve in tall glasses over crushed ice.

[026]
PRETTY IN PINK

Stay beautiful, inside and out, with this girly pink drink. You may not think of adding anything other than fruit to your juice, but wheatgerm is a girl's best friend when it comes to getting the most out of your smoothies, as the vitamin E in this tiny wheat seed helps to keep your skin in tip-top condition. Put all of the ingredients in your blender and whizz until smooth and creamy. Serve in two tall glasses.

250g/9oz STRAWBERRIES, hulled
2 BANANAS, peeled and cut into chunks
2 tsp WHEATGERM
100ml/3$^{1}/_{2}$ fl oz natural SOYA YOGHURT
300ml/10fl oz SOYA or nut MILK
fluffy towelling robe (optional)

[027]
CHOC BERRY

A rockin' 'n' rollin' blend of chocolate and strawberry, this thick milkshake tastes so good that you're bound to think it must be bad for you. But not so! Chocolate contains flavanoids, which protect you against disease, and strawberries are one of the richest sources of vitamin C. Blend the cocoa powder, milk and sugar with the strawberries and half the ice cream until the mixture is frothy and smooth. Pour into milkshake glasses, add a scoop of ice cream and sprinkle with chocolate. Bliss.

3 tsp good-quality COCOA powder
400ml/14fl oz semi-skimmed MILK
1–2 tsp caster SUGAR
300g/10½ oz STRAWBERRIES, hulled
4 scoops real dairy VANILLA ICE CREAM
2 squares good-quality plain CHOCOLATE, grated

2 BANANAS, peeled and cut into chunks
125ml/4fl oz natural BIO-YOGHURT
350ml/12fl oz semi-skimmed MILK
1 heaped tbsp smooth, sugar-free PEANUT BUTTER
$1/2$ tsp ground CINNAMON

[028]

MONKEY
NUT

This drink is for anyone who loves peanut butter and
banana sandwiches. What? They must be nuts! Try this
fabulous smoothie and you'll quickly understand the
appeal. This is a substantial and filling breakfast drink
that packs a protein punch to help sustain energy levels.
One glassful and you will be swinging from the trees,
albeit in the urban jungle … . Put all the ingredients
in your blender and whizz until smooth
and frothy. Serve in two tumblers.

2 BANANAS, peeled and cut into chunks
1 medium PINEAPPLE, peeled and chopped
300ml/10fl oz semi-skimmed MILK
2.5cm/1in piece fresh GINGER ROOT, peeled and grated,
or 2 tsp ginger cordial

[029]

MELLOW
YELLOW

Hey! This smoothie is far out, man. It's time to dig out that
floral kaftan, light a joss stick and prepare to abandon
yourself to a whole new experience. The taste sensation
created by this blend of creamy banana and sweet
pineapple, cut through with the spicy zing of ginger,
has to be experienced to be believed. Put all the
ingredients in your blender. Whizz until smooth and
creamy. Serve in two long glasses, with ice. Cool.

[030]
PEACH BABY

6 PEACHES, stoned and chopped
1 tsp VANILLA extract
4 scoops real dairy VANILLA ICE CREAM
300ml/10fl oz MILK
150ml/5fl oz GREEK YOGHURT
itsy bitsy polka-dot bikini (optional)

A holiday romance in a glass, this drink is the colour of sunset, and has a honeyed scent full of the promise of a balmy evening to come … . Peaches make a rich nectar that is completely irresistible when combined with vanilla. A ripe peach will yield to a gentle squeeze – as you may too, when the opportunity to do so presents itself! Blend everything together, but save a scoop of ice cream to drop into each glass just before serving.

[031]
CHOCO-BANANA -RAMA

120ml/8 tbsp natural SOYA YOGHURT
2 large BANANAS, peeled and cut into chunks
400ml/14fl oz SOYA or nut MILK
3 tsp good-quality COCOA powder (dairy-free)
2 tsp MAPLE SYRUP
grated NUTMEG, to serve

What a mouthful! Big and little kids alike will go bonkers for this creamy yet dairy-free banana and chocolate smoothie with its dollop of sticky maple syrup. Try to use pure maple syrup to get the authentic earthy flavour and, believe it or not, health benefits! Maple syrup actually contains fewer calories and has a higher concentration of minerals than honey. Blend all of the ingredients together until creamy. Pour into two tall glasses and sprinkle with grated nutmeg.

For a fab ice cream, mix this smoothie with an egg white and add 3 tbsps caster sugar. Pour into a container. Freeze for 2 hours and then whisk before returning to the freezer for another 2 hours. Repeat, then allow to freeze.

400g/14oz fresh RHUBARB, trimmed and cut into chunks
or 400g/14oz tinned rhubarb (drained weight)
2 tbsp caster SUGAR or to taste
150ml/5fl oz WATER
250ml/9fl oz ready-made CUSTARD
1 tsp VANILLA extract
200ml/7fl oz semi-skimmed MILK
your favourite comic (optional)

[032]

RHUBARB 'N' CUSTARD

Remember those delicious half-pink, half-yellow boiled sweets that you spent your pocket money on? Well, now you can enjoy a wave of candy-store nostalgia with this gorgeous smoothie. Put the fresh rhubarb (if using) in a saucepan with the sugar and water. Bring to the boil, reduce the heat and simmer, half-covered, until tender. Allow to cool. Put the cold, fresh (or tinned) rhubarb, custard, vanilla extract and milk in a blender and whizz until smooth and creamy. Serve in two large goblets.

[033]

TUTTI
FRUTTI

A tropical fruit crush that's guaranteed to transport you to sunnier climes after just one sip – but as you won't stop there, who knows where it will take you? Can't you just hear the palm trees gently swaying in the breeze and the waves lapping on the golden sands? To check in, blend the pineapple and the mango together. Press through a sieve to remove any fibres, then stir in the lime juice. Serve in two tall glasses, poured over crushed ice.

1 medium **PINEAPPLE**,
peeled and chopped
1 **MANGO**, peeled and sliced
1 tbsp freshly-squeezed **LIME** juice
crushed **ICE**, to serve
a hammock (optional)

100g/3^1/$_2$ oz RASPBERRIES
2 PEACHES, stoned and chopped
300ml/10fl oz semi-skimmed MILK
2 large scoops good-quality RASPBERRY RIPPLE ICE CREAM

[034]
PEACH MELBA

Do try and resist popping all the plump raspberries into your mouth the minute you get them home – saving a few for this smoothie will be well worth the self-discipline as something truly scrumptious happens when raspberries and peaches meet. Whizz the raspberries first and sieve them to remove the pips. Pour them back into the blender with the rest of the ingredients and whizz again to combine. Pour into glasses and take the time to enjoy!

1 AVOCADO, halved, stoned, peeled and sliced
1 CUCUMBER, peeled and cut into chunks
freshly-squeezed juice of 2 LIMES
300ml/10fl oz MILK
2 tbsp finely-chopped fresh CORIANDER
2 tbsp finely-chopped fresh MINT

GREEN [035]
GODDESS

By replacing the milk with the same quantity of vegetable stock you can
make a lovely chilled soup. Simply ladle into shallow bowls, swirl in a little
sour cream, and add slices of red chilli and more freshly-chopped coriander.

This savoury smoothie is made from an unusual
combination of ingredients, but it works a treat. It's
a sort of satin-smooth version of guacamole without the
garlic or spicy chillies. And as avocado is something of a
goddess nutritionally speaking, you would do well to
worship it for all the lovely things it's going to do for you,
both inside and out. Blend all the ingredients until they
take on a creamy consistency, and serve in tumblers.

Fruit crumble is the perfect comfort food and this delicious smoothie is the perfect drink to have during a cosy night in in front of the fire. Put the blackberries, juice and apples in your blender. Whizz until smooth, then press through a sieve to remove any pips. Return to the blender and add three-quarters of the toasted oats and the rest of the ingredients. Blend, pour into glasses and sprinkle with the remaining oats.

[036]
APPLE
CRUMBLE

150g/5$1/2$ oz canned BLACKBERRIES, drained,
but reserve 100ml/3$1/2$ fl oz of the juice
2 APPLES, peeled, cored and chopped
A handful of porridge OATS, toasted
100ml/3$1/2$ fl oz semi-skimmed MILK
100ml/3$1/2$ fl oz natural BIO-YOGHURT
$1/4$ tsp ground CINNAMON

[037]
COCO- CABANA

1 PAPAYA, peeled, deseeded and chopped
1/2 medium PINEAPPLE, peeled and chopped
200ml/7fl oz COCONUT MILK
120ml/8 tbsp natural BIO-YOGHURT
2 cocktail umbrellas (optional)

If you're a fan of the Piña Colada cocktail, then this is the drink for you. It's a sumptuous blend of papaya, pineapple and coconut with a truly tropical taste. As a bonus, pineapple is packed with a natural substance that keep joints flexible. Whizz the fruit with the coconut milk and the bio-yoghurt in a blender until smooth and creamy. Serve in two large goblets with ice and straws.

[038]

BLACK FOREST

200g/7oz tinned black CHERRIES
(drained weight)
4 purple PLUMS, stoned
and chopped
150ml /10 tbsp natural BIO-YOGHURT
1 tsp VANILLA extract
grated dark CHOCOLATE, to decorate

This drink pays homage to the gateau of the same name, which was popular in the 1970s. Juicing fresh cherries is a labour of love so it's easier to use tinned ones. A sexy, deep red colour, the chocolate and cherry combo works a treat. Blend the fruit, yoghurt and vanilla extract until smooth and creamy. Pour into tall glasses and sprinkle with grated chocolate.
Grrrr … easy tiger!

[039]

DREAM DATE

150g/5$1/2$ oz dried, stoned,
ready-to-eat DATES, roughly chopped
300ml/10fl oz WATER
120ml/8 tbsp natural BIO-YOGHURT
1 tsp VANILLA extract
300ml/10fl oz semi-skimmed MILK
fab new shoes (optional)

Lucky in love? You are bound to form a lasting relationship with this velvety drink. Dates can't be juiced, but they are perfect in smoothies. Put the dates in a saucepan and cover them with water. Bring to the boil, reduce the heat, cover and simmer for 10 minutes, until they are tender. When cool, put them and any remaining water in the blender with the rest of the ingredients. Whizz until smooth, pour into tall glasses and serve.

8 LAVENDER flower heads
2 tbsp caster SUGAR
200ml/7fl oz WATER
350g/12oz mixed BERRIES, such as
strawberries, raspberries,
blueberries and blackcurrants
crushed ICE, to serve

[040]

FRENCH BERRY

Ooh la la! This is something very special. The addition of fragrant lavender gives this berry crush real sophistication. Put the flowers in a saucepan with the sugar and water. Bring to the boil, stirring until the sugar has dissolved. Remove from the heat and leave to infuse for 10 minutes. Blend the berries, then press through a sieve to remove pips. Strain the lavender syrup into the berry juice and stir well. Pour into tall glasses filled with crushed ice, and serve.

Tangy, icy, pure and invigorating ...
nothing beats a freshly-prepared
juice served over ice for instant
refreshment on a hot and
sticky summer's day.

[COOLERS AND
QUENCHERS]

Searching for a healthier alternative to the traditional
ice-cold beer? Then look no further. In this lifesaving
chapter you'll find some seriously smart ideas for
coolers and quenchers, all perfect for days when the
going gets hot. Before you start, make sure you've got
plenty of ice cubes and good fruit sorbets in your
freezer, because you'll be crushing and blending
ice with every summer fruit from citrus to
tropical, and adding a generous dollop of
sorbet to lots of the juices, too.

225g/8oz pearl BARLEY
1.7 litres/3 pints WATER
grated rind of 1 large unwaxed LEMON
55g/2oz golden caster SUGAR
freshly-squeezed
juice of 4 LEMONS
ball boys (optional)

[041]
OLD-FASHIONED
LEMON BARLEY

Anyone for tennis? This quintessentially British drink is easy to make and offers a welcome alternative to additive-laden squashes. Rinse the pearl barley in cold water and put into a large saucepan. Cover with the water and bring to the boil. Reduce the heat and simmer for 25 minutes, skimming off any froth from the surface. Remove from the heat. Add the lemon rind and sugar, and stir until the sugar has dissolved. Once cool, strain into a jug that can hold 1.7 litres/3 pints, and discard the barley. Add the lemon juice, taste and add more sugar if necessary, then serve.

[042] COOL AS A CUCUMBER

No other juice blend quite hits the spot like this one on a sticky summer's day. Watermelon is bursting with refreshment and it is a great rehydrator for the body. Although lovely and cooling, cucumber doesn't usually have a notable flavour, but it becomes surprisingly tasty when blended. This juice is best drunk through a straw, from a long, ice-filled glass – preferably while relaxing on a roof terrace. Put the watermelon and cucumber through a juicer. Pour into long, ice-filled glasses and serve with sprigs of mint.

1/2 medium **WATERMELON**, peeled and cut into wedges
1 medium **CUCUMBER**, cut into long wedges
ICE, to serve
sprigs of fresh **MINT**, to decorate

3 ORANGES, halved
1 medium PINEAPPLE, peeled and
chopped
300ml/10fl oz SODA WATER
ICE, to serve
2 slices ORANGE, to decorate
a camel (optional)

SAHARA [043]
SUNSET

Here's a thirst quencher fit for desert duty – just the thing you'd want to find waiting for you in the cool of a Bedouin tent after a day in the blistering heat. No? Oh, Brad Pitt it is then … . Use a citrus press or reamer to juice the oranges. Combine the orange juice with the juiced pineapple and pour into two glasses. Top up with soda and stir well. Add ice and a slice of orange to each one.

[044]

St CLEMENT'S SODA

1 red GRAPEFRUIT, halved
3 ORANGES, halved
2 scoops LEMON SORBET
chilled sparkling MINERAL WATER,
to serve

This is a blend of bitter grapefruit
and sweet orange served soda fountain-
style in a tall glass with lemon sorbet.
It's the ultimate in citrus refreshment
and a grown-up way to enjoy the retro
treat of a fruit sherbet. Use a citrus
press or reamer to juice the fruits.
Pour the juice into two highball
glasses. Add a scoop of lemon sorbet
to each glass and top up with sparkling
water, before serving with straws and
long-handled spoons.

GAZPACHO IN A
[045]
GLASS

300ml/10fl oz chilled WATER
450g/1lb vine-ripened TOMATOES, deseeded
1 small CUCUMBER, peeled, and cut into chunks
1/2 red PEPPER, deseeded and sliced
1 clove GARLIC, crushed
1 tbsp extra-virgin OLIVE OIL
1 mild green CHILLI, chopped finely
freshly-squeezed juice of 1 LEMON
a few drops of TABASCO
SALT and PEPPER

You'll be familiar with Gazpacho, the Spanish chilled soup made with tomatoes, garlic and olive oil, served with finely chopped vegetable trimmings. The same Mediterranean flavours go into this satisfying savoury smoothie – perfect with a salad lunch alfresco. Place all of the ingredients (except the Tabasco and seasoning) in a blender. Whizz until puréed, then season with salt, pepper and Tabasco to taste. Serve poured over ice.

1 large **MANGO**, peeled and sliced
300g/10$\frac{1}{2}$ oz **RASPBERRIES**
2 large scoops of **MANGO SORBET**
crushed **ICE**, to serve

[046]
RUBY
TUESDAY

Contrary to its name, this isn't a juice that can be enjoyed only on one day of the week. It's called Ruby Tuesday because, as the Rolling Stones say, "Catch your dreams before they slip away ..." or, in this case, eat the sorbet before it melts into the velvety fruit purée underneath. Sound advice. Juice the fruit. Pour the juice into two glasses and add a ball of sorbet to each. Top up with crushed ice and serve with long spoons.

[047]
FRUIT FLOAT

2 PEACHES, stoned and chopped
3 PLUMS, stoned and chopped
4 large scoops of real dairy VANILLA ICE CREAM
chilled SODA WATER, to serve

Remember the ice-cream floats you had as a child? Well, here's a healthy, grown-up version that positively bursts with fruitiness, making the most of the way sweet peaches mingle with the tang of plums. Put both fruits in a blender and whizz. Scoop the fruit pulp into two big glasses. Add two scoops of ice cream to each glass, top up with soda water, and serve.

2 LIMES, halved
1 LEMON, halved
2 tbsp finely-chopped fresh MINT
$1/2$ tsp caster SUGAR
chilled SODA WATER and crushed ICE, to serve
slices of LIME to decorate

VIRGIN [048] MOJITO

Why not try an alcoholic version of this drink? It's the perfect wind-down on a hot summer's evening. Just leave out the lemon juice, add a shot of cachaça or white rum to each glass, and serve with a swizzle stick.

The refreshing menthol ingredient in mint is perfect for drinks made in the world's hot spots, such as Cuba, home of the deliciously minty Mojito cocktail. This is a non-alcoholic version in which the traditional rum is left out. Use a citrus press or reamer to juice the fruit into a jug. Stir in the mint and the sugar. Divide between two large glasses and top up with tonic water. Add crushed ice and a slice of lime to each glass, and serve.

200g/7oz PINEAPPLE, peeled and chopped
2.5cm/1in piece fresh GINGER ROOT, peeled and grated
chilled GINGER ALE, to serve

PINEAPPLE [049] ZINGER

If you like sour-sweet flavours, then give this frozen cooler a try. Fresh ginger root has a hot, spicy pungency that cuts right through the sugariness of fruit and creates something with real bite. Delicious. Finely chop the pineapple in a blender or food processor. Combine with the ginger and spoon into a small freezer-proof container. Freeze for 2 hours. Mix to break up the ice crystals, then divide between two tall glasses. Top up with ginger ale and serve.

[050]
ROSEBERRY

300g/10¹/₂ oz summer BERRIES,
including strawberries, raspberries
and blueberries, hulled if necessary
¹/₂ tsp ROSEWATER
1 tbsp runny HONEY
chilled sparkling MINERAL WATER
ICE, to serve
time to daydream (optional)

In this drink summer berries
are blended with honey and a little
rosewater, which adds a lovely, subtle
floral taste. This is the drink that warm
evenings, verandahs and swing chairs
were created for. Purée the berries in
a blender. Press through a sieve into
a jug to remove the pips, if preferred.
Add the rosewater and honey to the
berries and mix well. Divide between
two tall glasses. Top up with sparkling
water and ice, and serve.

300g/10$\frac{1}{2}$ oz STRAWBERRIES, hulled
1 BANANA, peeled and cut into chunks
8 ICE cubes, crushed
100ml/3$\frac{1}{2}$ fl oz freshly-squeezed
ORANGE juice
2 large scoops ORANGE SORBET

[051]

FEELING
FRUITY

In the words of Carmen Miranda, "I, I, I, I like it verrrry much!" This drink is worth making a song and a dance about. An ice-blended fruit salad topped with a ball of orange sorbet – a truly fruity and refreshing experience that's hard to beat. Add the fruit to the blender along with the ice and the orange juice, and whizz until smooth. Divide between two glasses and add a scoop of sorbet to each one. Serve with long spoons.

To make a fantastic summer treat known as Monkey Tails, dip frozen bananas into good-quality melted chocolate (milk or dark) and leave to cool and harden before threading onto sticks and eating like ice lollies. Delicious !

[052]

BANOFFI
FREEZE

2 BANANAS, peeled, wrapped in clingfilm and frozen
$1/2$ tsp ground CINNAMON
300ml/10fl oz SOYA or nut milk
1 tbsp MAPLE SYRUP

This delicious smoothie is inspired by Banoffi Pie, the hugely popular dessert. The clever thing here is that the bananas are frozen before being blended so that they take on an ice-creamy texture. The maple syrup adds a toffee-like taste and using soya or nut milk means that you get a creamy frozen milkshake that's non-dairy. Genius. Put the frozen bananas in a blender with the rest of the ingredients. Blend until smooth, then serve.

[053]
PURPLE HAZE

2 PEARS, peeled, cored and chopped
1 APPLE, peeled, cored and chopped
100g/3$1/2$ oz frozen BLUEBERRIES
1 tbsp runny HONEY
chilled sparkling MINERAL WATER, to serve

Difficult though it may be, sacrifice a ripe, juicy pear to your blender. You will be very glad that you did once you have tasted this heavenly concoction. Apple and pears are natural taste partners, so what gives this cordial-style juice both its edge and its moody purple hue is the addition of blueberries. Blend the prepared fruit with the frozen blueberries and honey. Divide the purée between two tall glasses and top up with sparkling water before serving.

1cm/$1/2$ in piece of fresh GINGER ROOT, peeled
1 honeydew MELON, peeled, deseeded and cut
into wedges
2 large scoops MELON SORBET
chilled sparkling MINERAL WATER, to serve

[054]

GINGER

SWINGER

Melon and ginger is a classic taste combination but this fragrant smoothie is a long way from the melon balls sprinkled with dry ginger that were a regular fixture at 70s' parties. Melon takes on a velvety texture when it's juiced, and adding spicy fresh ginger makes this a modern taste sensation. Juice the melon with the peeled ginger. Pour the juice into two large glasses. Add a ball of sorbet to each glass, top up with sparkling water and serve.

1 small LEMON, halved
2 green or white TEA bags
500ml/18fl oz boiling WATER
1 BAY leaf
ICE and LEMON slices, to serve
ancient wisdom (optional)

GREEN [055]
DRAGON

A deliciously simple drink to prepare and a health-
enhancing one too, as green tea is full of antioxidants.
Definitely one for fans of iced lemon tea to try. Squeeze
the juice from the lemon using a citrus press or a reamer.
Put the tea bags into a jug and pour in boiling water;
leave to steep for 2 minutes, then remove the tea bags.
Add the bay leaf and leave to cool. Transfer to the fridge
to chill, remove the bay leaf and add the lemon juice.
Serve with ice and a slice of lemon.

TWO TO MANGO

[056]

1 large MANGO, peeled and sliced
4 scoops of MANGO SORBET
freshly-squeezed juice of 1 LIME
ICE, to serve

Mango is one of the most sumptuous fruits. It has sticky and sweet flesh so juicy that you feel you just have to share it with someone you care about. This dramatic blend of mango, mango sorbet and lime juice will have you dancing with a rose between your teeth in no time! Put the mango in your blender and whizz until puréed. Add the mango sorbet and lime juice, and blend until slushy. Serve with ice.

To make a delicious and elegant summer punch add a splash of citron vodka to this drink and serve in a large pitcher, topped up with soda water or lemonade and with slices of orange and lemon.

[057]
SUMMER WINE

300g/10$\frac{1}{2}$ oz frozen mixed SUMMER FRUIT, such as cherries,
blueberries, blackberries and blackcurrants
400ml/14fl oz freshly-squeezed ORANGE juice
HONEY or sugar to taste
ICE cubes, to serve
2 slices of ORANGE, to garnish

This blend of soft summer fruits creates an intoxicatingly rich juice that is a deep, dark claret colour, reminiscent of a glass of wine. To make, simply put the fruit and orange juice in your blender and whizz. Taste a little and add a few spoonfuls of honey or sugar if it is too tart. Serve in two large wine glasses with ice and slices of orange.

6 ICE cubes, crushed
2 APPLES, stalks removed, and quartered
300ml/10fl oz CRANBERRY juice (unsweetened)
freshly-squeezed LEMON juice, to taste
100ml/3$1/2$ fl oz sparkling MINERAL WATER

[058]

LOVE APPLE

This refreshing spritzer gets its distinctive,
bittersweet taste from cranberry juice. Cranberries
are also known as bounceberries because the
traditional test for firmness was to bounce them
seven times and discard any that were too squashy
to make the grade! How loveable is that? Divide
the ice between two glasses. Juice the apples and
combine them with the other juices. Pour into tall
glasses and top up with mineral water. Stir and
serve with ice and straws.

TROPICAL [059]
TWIST

1 small PINEAPPLE, peeled,
chopped, and frozen
3 PEACHES, stoned and chopped
freshly-squeezed LIME
juice, to taste
chilled sparkling MINERAL
WATER, to serve
strips of LIME zest, to decorate

This is a playful little juice with an intriguing sour-sweet
tang. Crush the frozen pineapple in a blender (if your
blender can't manage frozen fruit, allow the pineapple to
defrost partially first). Add the peaches and lime juice, then
blend until they form a thick nectar. Divide between two
tall glasses and top up with fizzy mineral water.
Add a twist of lime zest before serving.

[060]
SUNRISE

This is the drink for anyone who has ever stayed up all night to watch the sun rise from behind the ocean. And as if the sublime colour isn't enough on its own, this proven flavour combination uses raspberry sorbet, rather than fruit, to give the drink a truly sensational sherbety quality. Use a citrus press or reamer to juice the oranges. Blend with the sorbet. Pour the fruit slush into two highball glasses and top up with sparkling water. Decorate with mint sprigs before serving.

6 ORANGES, halved
2 large scoops of RASPBERRY SORBET
chilled sparkling MINERAL WATER, to serve
2 small sprigs fresh MINT, to decorate

**Sharp, clean, reviving and cleansing ...
the right juice is perfect for boosting
flagging energy levels and giving a
sluggish system a healthy kick-start.**

PICK-ME-UPS AND
REVIVERS

Is the hectic pace of modern life getting to you? Feeling
worn out and exhausted? Skin dull, digestion sluggish,
do you seem to be endlessly fighting a cold? If so, you
need some juice therapy, and fast! Fruit and veggies
are nature's pick-me-ups and revivers – because they're
packed with essential vitamins and minerals plus other
health-enhancing substances that can do so much: boost
your energy levels, clear your complexion, calm your
tummy and strengthen your immune system. In this
chapter you'll find a juice pharmacy offering delicious
and effective remedies for everyday ills.

85g/3oz white GRAPES
2.5cm/1in piece fresh GINGER ROOT, peeled
1 raw BEETROOT, trimmed and cut into chunks
1 APPLE, stalk removed, and quartered
1 CARROT, chopped
freshly-squeezed juice of 1 LEMON
blushes (optional)

[061] MORNING AFTER

Ouch … poor you. Sore head, dry mouth and upset tummy? Never mind, you probably had a great evening, and help is here in this combination of liver-cleansing and rejuvenating fruit and veggies. Ginger is known to relieve nausea and settle the stomach, while beetroot is one of the most mineral-rich, blood-boosting tonics there is. Juice the grapes, ginger, beetroot, apple and carrot, stir in the lemon juice, drink and start to feel human again.

[062] CLEANSE 'N' TONE

Not just pretty faces, juicy little grapes are also nature's most potent cleansers. They are highly nutritious – containing natural sugars, potassium, iron and fibre – and have a detoxifying effect on the body, helping to improve the condition of your skin. Adding melon gives this beauty-boosting blend its body and extra sweetness. Just juice the melon and the grapes, add the lemon juice, and serve.

1/2 Cantaloupe MELON, peeled, deseeded
and cut into wedges
200g/7oz black seedless GRAPES
freshly-squeezed juice of 1 LEMON

[063]
STRESSBUSTER

250g/9oz STRAWBERRIES, hulled
2 medium CARROTS, chopped
3 APRICOTS, stoned and chopped
2 ORANGES, halved
a punch bag (optional)

Living your life at a hectic pace? Worn out, ragged, stressed? Here is the perfect antidote – a juice packed with vitamin C, beta-carotene and B-vitamins that helps to reduce anxiety and tension. As a bonus, it also delivers a good dose of antioxidants that can boost a flagging immune system – another major symptom of stress. Juice the strawberries, carrots and apricots. Use a citrus press or reamer to squeeze the juice from the oranges. Mix everything together, serve and … r-e-l-a-x.

If you really can't face a green drink, don't worry. You can still give this juice a nutritional leg-up by leaving out the spirulina and adding a couple of teaspoonfuls of flaxseeds, which are another rich source of vitamins, minerals and essential fatty acids.

[064]

STAY WELL

Don't be put of by the murky green, slightly swamp-like appearance of this tasty juice. Spirulina is a "wonder food", rich in beta-carotene, iron, vitamin B-12 and the essential fatty acid, GLA. This means that it's bursting with nutrients that will keep your immune system fighting fit and keep you healthy. Juice the carrots, pears and grapes. Mix the spirulina with a little of the juice, then stir the paste into the rest of the juice until combined. Serve straightaway.

3 medium CARROTS, chopped
2 PEARS, stalks removed, and quartered
150g/5^1/$_2$ oz white seedless GRAPES
2 tsp powdered SPIRULINA

BREATHE EASY
[065]

3 tsp ELDERFLOWER CORDIAL
400ml/14fl oz hot WATER
1 tsp runny HONEY
4 CLOVES
2 APPLES, peeled, cored and chopped
115g/4oz tinned BLACKCURRANTS (drained weight)
a day in bed (optional)

Ah … choo! Got a nasty cold? Take to your bed with a box of tissues, a pile of magazines and a glassful of this spicy, vitamin-C packed juice. Pour the elderflower cordial into a heatproof jug and add the hot water. Stir in the honey and cloves and leave to cool. Put the apples and blackcurrants into a blender and purée. Add the fruit purée to the cordial mixture and stir well. Remove the cloves before serving.

[066] WINTER WARMER

2 tsp runny HONEY
300ml/10fl oz hot WATER
4 KIWI FRUITS, peeled and
quartered
freshly-squeezed juice of
1 LEMON
2.5cm/1in piece of fresh
GINGER ROOT, peeled
grated NUTMEG, to serve

A woolly hat, scarf and gloves, and this juice –
all you need to keep warm and well on a cold
winter's day. It's packed with germ-fighting
vitamin C, antiseptic honey, and circulation-
boosting ginger. Stir the honey into the hot
water until dissolved and leave to cool. Juice the
kiwi fruits and ginger. Add the lemon juice and
cooled honey water, stir and pour into glasses.
Sprinkle with grated nutmeg before serving.

2 APPLES, stalks removed, and quartered
1 small CUCUMBER, cut into long wedges
1 small FENNEL bulb, cut into long wedges
1/4 medium red CABBAGE, sliced
1 red PEPPER, deseeded and sliced
freshly-squeezed LEMON juice, to taste

GIRL [067]
POWER

Don't be put off by this unusual combination
of vegetable and fruit ingredients – when
blended together these juices make a serious
nutritional heavyweight, albeit one disguised
as a girly pink drink! Packed with vitamins
and minerals, including immunity-boosting
antioxidants, this is a well-muscled glassful.
Juice the apples, cucumber, fennel, cabbage
and red pepper. Add a squeeze of lemon juice,
mix the juices well until combined and serve.

To make this delicious iced tea even more special you can add a measure of the French apple brandy Calvados to turn it into a warming and scrummy winter nightcap.

300ml/10fl oz just boiled WATER
1 white TEA bag or equivalent amount of loose tea
2 APPLES, stalks removed, and quartered
freshly-squeezed juice of 1 LEMON
ICE cubes, to serve
LEMON slices, to serve

[068]
APPLE TEA

The bitter flavour of tea works well with the sweetness of apples here to make an ultra-refreshing drink. White tea is thought to reduce the harmful effects of free radicals in the body. Immerse the tea bag or leaves in the water. Infuse for 3 minutes, then remove the tea bag or strain the leaves, and leave the tea to cool. Juice the apples and mix with the lemon juice and cold tea. Serve with ice and lemon slices.

ADIOS AMIGOS!
[069]

55g/2oz WATERCRESS
large handful fresh PARSLEY
1 APPLE, stalks removed, and quartered
3 medium CARROTS, chopped
freshly-squeezed LEMON juice, to taste

Too old for spots? It's time to wave goodbye to unsightly blemishes once and for all. Liver-cleansing apple is mixed with beta-carotene-rich carrots to create a juice that's a force to reckoned with in the fight against acne. Peppery watercress gives an interesting edge to this otherwise sweet juice. Gather the watercress and the parsley into a bundle and juice with the apple and carrots. Add a squeeze of lemon juice before serving.

3 medium CARROTS, chopped
1 CELERY stick
2 raw BEETROOT, trimmed and cut into chunks
freshly-squeezed juice of 1 LEMON
2 tsp WHEATGRASS powder

INSTANT
DETOX
[070]

Find the idea of a full-on detox rather daunting? Here's the solution: an effective, detoxifying juice made from nature's most effective cleansers and diuretics to help to eliminate toxins and restore your liver to its former glory. Juice the carrots, celery and beetroot, and mix with the lemon juice. Mix the wheatgrass powder with a small amount of the juice, and stir this paste into the rest of the juice. Combine and serve immediately.

8 vine-ripened **TOMATOES**,
halved if large
2 medium **CARROTS**, chopped
1 stick **CELERY**
1 mild fresh red **CHILLI**, deseeded
1 tsp **WORCESTERSHIRE** sauce
ICE, to serve

GET HAPPY [071]

We all get a little down in the dumps from time to time, so here is a juice that can really help to put a smile back on your face. The spicy heat of chillies on the tongue causes the release of endorphins, the body's natural painkillers, which encourage a feeling of well-being and happiness. Simply put the tomatoes, carrots, celery and chilli through the juicer. Add the Worcestershire sauce and serve with ice.

CLEVER
CLOGS
[072]

Want to wow your boss? Or win a million on TV? Or just remember where you put the car keys … ? The almonds and sunflower seeds in this lovely, thick banana and yoghurt blend are rich in memory-boosting B-vitamins, Omega-6 fatty acids and zinc. Put the almonds and sunflower seeds in a blender and process until very finely ground. Add the bananas, milk, yoghurt and cinnamon, whizz until smooth and creamy, and serve.

55g/2oz shelled ALMONDS
2 tbsp SUNFLOWER seeds
2 BANANAS, peeled and cut into chunks
300ml/10fl oz semi-skimmed MILK
90ml/6 tbsp natural BIO-YOGHURT
1/2 tsp ground CINNAMON

[073]
C MAJOR

This fresh and tangy juice is bursting at the seams with health-enhancing super-vitamin C, thanks to the presence of both blueberries and cranberries. Vitamin C is a highly effective antioxidant, and making sure that you get lots of it can reduce the risk of becoming ill, as it helps to boost and protect the immune system. Simplicity itself to make, just juice the blueberries and apples. Combine them with the cranberry juice, mix well and serve.

150g/5$\frac{1}{2}$oz BLUEBERRIES
2 APPLES, stalks removed,
and quartered
300ml/10fl oz CRANBERRY juice

300g/10$^{1}/_{2}$ oz STRAWBERRIES, hulled
2 medium CARROTS, chopped
2 blood ORANGES, halved
20 drops ECHINACEA

[074]

COLD ZAPPER

Strawberries are not only delicious but they are also packed with vitamin C. Combine them with echinacea – a herbal extract that's thought to protect against the cold virus and to reduce the time that colds last – and you've got the best possible defence against the worst of the winter germs. Put the strawberries and the carrots through the juicer. Use a citrus press or reamer to squeeze the juice from the oranges. Mix together the juices, add the echinacea and serve immediately.

[075]
GREEN GIANT

100g/3$\frac{1}{2}$ oz WATERCRESS
250g/9oz BROCCOLI stalks
1 large CUCUMBER, halved lengthways
freshly-squeezed juice of 1 LIME
ICE, to serve

This giant of a juice is positively bursting out of its shirt
with goodness. Vitamins, minerals and phytonutrients
all mingle in a refreshing and tasty drink that is
packed full of antioxidants, and immunity-boosting
and anti-carcinogenic substances. Form the watercress
into a bundle and put through the juicer with the broccoli
and the cucumber. Add the lime juice, stir well and serve
immediately with ice.

This makes a lovely finish to a hot and spicy meal. To make a dessert similar to the Indian ice cream kulfi, pour it into small shot glasses and pop in the freezer for about half an hour before serving with small spoons.

2 BANANAS, peeled and cut into chunks
1 small PINEAPPLE, peeled and chopped
2.5cm/1in piece fresh GINGER ROOT, peeled and grated
300ml/10fl oz semi-skimmed MILK
120ml/8 tbsp natural BIO-YOGHURT

YUMMY
[076]
TUMMY

Tummy playing up? This deliciously creamy drink contains fibre-rich bananas, as well as pineapple, which has an alkaline substance called bromelain that works like an indigestion tablet to settle the stomach. The addition of natural bio-yoghurt with its "friendly" bacteria, and ginger, to relieve nausea, makes this a glassful that will restore order in no time. Put the bananas, pineapple, ginger, milk and yoghurt into a blender, whizz until smooth and creamy, and serve.

1 round LETTUCE, halved
250g/9oz BROCCOLI stalks
2 APPLES, stalks removed and quartered
freshly-squeezed juice of 1 LEMON
a good book (optional)

[077]
SLEEPYHEAD

The pace of daily life can make getting to sleep harder than
it should be. If your mind is still working overtime and you
need extra help, try a glass of this tried-and-tested natural
remedy because lettuce contains a substance said to have
sleep-inducing properties. Form the lettuce into a bundle
and juice with the broccoli stalks and apples.
Add the lemon juice and serve.

[078] BRIGHT
EYES

1 MANGO, peeled and sliced
300g/10$^1/_2$ oz mixed BERRIES of your choice,
including blueberries
120ml/8 tbsp natural BIO-YOGHURT
200ml/7fl oz semi-skimmed MILK
an early night (optional)

Lost your sparkle? Late nights,
computer screens and pollution can
all play havoc with your best feature.
Here's a treat that not only tastes divine,
but is packed with nutrients that help
to keep your eyes healthy and beautiful.
Put the mango and berries in a blender
with the yoghurt and milk, and whizz
until smooth and creamy.
Serve in tall glasses.

CLEAN
[079] SWEEP

2 APPLES, stalks removed, and quartered
2 PEARS, stalks removed, and quartered
chilled PRUNE juice
1 tbsp freshly-squeezed LEMON juice

Every now and then the body benefits from a thorough internal cleanse. This juice does the job as it contains both apples, known as "the body's broom" in complementary medicine, and prunes, which are a good source of fibre. Juice the apples and pears and pour into a measuring jug. Add sufficient prune juice to make the liquid up to 600ml/1 pint. Stir in the lemon juice and mix well before serving in two tall glasses.

BEET
[080] BOOSTER

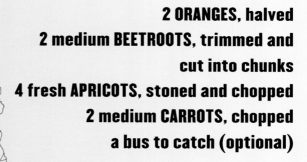

2 ORANGES, halved
2 medium BEETROOTS, trimmed and
cut into chunks
4 fresh APRICOTS, stoned and chopped
2 medium CARROTS, chopped
a bus to catch (optional)

This eye-poppingly different drink
will give you a tasty energy lift. It's
packed with vitamin C, which helps
your body to turn food into energy,
plus encourages the absorption of iron –
a great lethargy fighter. Use a citrus
press or reamer to squeeze the juice from
the oranges. Juice the beetroots, apricots
and carrots, then mix with the fresh
orange juice. Pour into two long glasses.
Drink, and you'll be raring to go!

Smooth, cool, sophisticated and indulgent ... sometimes the only way to unwind is to enjoy a luxurious drink with just a hint of the strong stuff.

[TIPPLES]

Had a tough day at work? Deserve a treat? Celebrating a special occasion? Whatever your reason, you will find some truly grown-up ways to indulge yourself and to enjoy the heady pleasures of alcoholic drinks in this chapter. What's more, you can be secure in the knowledge that you are still benefiting from all the great things that juices can do for you! Champagne and juice cocktails, vodka coolers, summer punches and Margaritas are all included here to tickle your taste buds and stimulate your senses.

**85g/3oz RASPBERRIES
1 PEACH, stoned and chopped
1 tbsp caster SUGAR
CHAMPAGNE or Cava, to serve**

[081]
MELBA FIZZ

This pretty and sticky-sweet summer Champagne cocktail brings together the classic fruit combination of peaches and raspberries to create a perfect aperitif, ideal for sipping on a warm summer's evening. Simple to make, start by blending together the raspberries, peach and sugar. Force the purée through a fine sieve to remove any raspberry pips and then divide it between two small wine glasses or Champagne flutes before topping up with chilled fizz. Stir and serve. Heavenly.

$^{1}/_{2}$ small **WATERMELON, peeled and cut into wedges**
2 large measures VODKA
1 tbsp finely-chopped fresh MINT
ICE, to serve

[082]

WATERMELON
COOLER

Fresh mint is bursting with zingy natural menthol that creates an instant sensation of freshness in your mouth, which is why it's a popular ingredient in cooling cocktails, such as the classic Mint Julep. Blended here with succulent watermelon, it creates a drink that's pure refreshment in a glass. Juice the watermelon and pour into a jug. Stir in the vodka and pour the drink into two tumblers. Add the mint, stir well, and top up with ice.

2 ORANGES, halved
1 PASSION fruit, halved
CHAMPAGNE or Cava
Someone special (optional)

[083]
PURE
PASSION

If you are fond of Buck's Fizz, the classic brunch tipple, you'll be crazy in love with the sophisticated taste that comes from adding the sour-sweet flesh of passion fruit in this version. Use a citrus press or reamer to juice the oranges. Scoop the pulp and edible seeds out of the passion fruit and stir them into the orange juice. Pour the juice into two Champagne flutes and top up with chilled Champagne or cava.

[084]
AL FRESCO

55g/2oz RASPBERRIES
1 tbsp caster SUGAR
25ml/1fl oz COINTREAU
CHAMPAGNE or Cava

Adding a splash of fruit-based liqueur
gives any juice cocktail a real lift. The
fresh tastes of raspberry and orange
work beautifully here with the fizz
to create a refreshing and sherbety
summer drink. Purée the raspberries
in a blender. Force the purée through
a sieve to remove the seeds. Spoon it
into a jug and stir in the sugar and
the Cointreau. Pour into two wine
glasses or Champagne flutes and top
up with chilled Champagne or cava.

100g/3$^{1}/_{2}$ oz STRAWBERRIES, hulled
2 ORANGES, halved
1 tsp caster SUGAR
2 large measures GIN
crushed ICE, to serve

[085]
JUICY GIN

The essence of summertime is captured
in this blend of succulent strawberries
combined with the distinctive flavour of
gin – perfect for sipping while you watch the
croquet. Purée the strawberries in a blender.
Use a citrus press or reamer to squeeze the
juice from the oranges. Mix the fruit with
the sugar and gin in a jug. Pour into two
small wine glasses and top up with crushed
ice before serving.

SORRENTO
SPARKLER
[086]

2 ORANGES, halved
1 small LEMON, halved
1 measure LIMONCELLO
2 large measures VODKA
chilled, sparkling MINERAL WATER, to serve
slices of ORANGE, to decorate

Limoncello is the magic ingredient in this sparkling citrus refresher. It's a delicious golden-yellow Italian liqueur that's traditionally served in tiny, freezer-frosted glasses as a digestive. Use a citrus press or reamer to squeeze the juice from the oranges and lemon. Stir in the Limoncello and vodka before pouring into two highball glasses. Add a few ice cubes, top up with fizzy water and serve with slices of orange.

While you've got the Limoncello out make the most of it! Stir a little into fresh double cream – it's gorgeous dolloped onto a bowl of strawberries. Or serve it Sorrento-style, neat and straight from the freezer in shot glasses.

[087] MANGO
DAIQUIRI

8 ICE cubes, crushed
1 large MANGO, peeled and sliced
2 large measures white RUM
freshly-squeezed juice of 1 LIME
1 tsp caster SUGAR
a panama hat (optional)

A daiquiri is a classic cocktail from Havana, but why travel all the way to Cuba when you can whizz up your own ice-blended, creamy mango and rum cooler at home? Put the ice, mango, rum, lime juice and sugar in the blender and whizz until combined. Pour into two large goblets and serve.

6 ICE cubes, crushed
1 medium PINEAPPLE, peeled and chopped
100ml/3$1/2$ fl oz COCONUT MILK
2 large measures white RUM
freshly-squeezed juice of 1 LIME
1 tsp SUGAR

FRESH [088]
COLADA

Piña Colada just had to be included here – it's the most
popular fruit cocktail ever created. True to the spirit of
juicing, this recipe uses fresh pineapple juice to give the
drink a refreshing tang. Put the ice, pineapple, coconut
milk, rum, lime juice and sugar into your blender,
then whizz until frothy and creamy. Serve in
two large goblets with straws.

200g/7oz white seedless GRAPES
350ml/12fl oz dry white
WINE, chilled
chilled SODA WATER
LEMON slices, to serve

[089]
GRAPE TWIST

Want to try a new version of the classic spritzer? By adding a handful of juicy grapes to the simple blend of white wine and soda, you can turn this humble glassful into a first-class thirst-quencher. You don't need to use expensive wine – a basic one will do the job nicely. Juice the grapes, put them in a jug and add the wine. Pour into two ice-filled highball glasses, top up with a splash of soda and add slices of lemon.

[090]
OCEAN BREEZE

Here's one to make your taste buds tingle. It's similar to the classic Sea Breeze, only made with pink grapefruit rather than white. This makes a delectably pink drink with a sharp, tangy flavour that comes as something of a surprise – and a very welcome one! Use a citrus press or reamer to squeeze the juice from the grapefruit. Combine with the vodka and pour into two ice-filled highball glasses. Top up with cranberry juice and serve.

1 pink GRAPEFRUIT, halved
2 large measures VODKA
ICE, to serve
CRANBERRY juice

As a cool alternative, try blending the apple with cucumber instead of blackcurrants. This creates a pale and interesting drink with a subtle, refreshing flavour. There's no need to peel the cucumber – just wash and chop it before blending.

2 APPLES, peeled, cored and quartered
115g/4oz tinned BLACKCURRANTS (drained weight)
2 large measures PIMM'S
chilled SODA WATER
ICE, to serve

[091]
MIDNIGHT PIMM'S

A twist on the summer classic of Pimm's and lemonade, this version uses tart apples and blackcurrants to make a fruity alternative to the rather sugary classic. Blend the apples (keeping $\frac{1}{2}$ apple to decorate) with the blackcurrants, then add the Pimm's and blend again. Pour the fruit purée into two highball glasses and top up with soda water. Thinly slice the reserved apple and add to the glasses with ice.

A truly elegant drink inspired by the classic Italian Bellini – a blend of white peach juice and Prosecco that was created at the legendary Harry's Bar in Venice. Definitely made for lazy afternoons and beautiful people – which includes you, naturally. Juice the peaches and combine the liquid with the peach schnapps, then stir in the sugar. Pour the fruit mixture into two Champagne flutes and top up with chilled bubbly or Cava.

[092]
DOLCE VITA

4 PEACHES, stoned and chopped
2 measures peach SCHNAPPS
1 tsp caster SUGAR
CHAMPAGNE or Cava
Champagne lifestyle (optional)

115g/4oz canned BLACKBERRIES (drained weight)
2 large measures GIN
1 tbsp CRÈME DE CASSIS liqueur
4 ICE cubes, plus extra to serve
100ml/3$\frac{1}{2}$ fl oz fresh APPLE juice

[093]

BRAMBLE

Lovely plump blackberries give this seriously fruity tipple
its intense flavour – one that's accentuated by the crème de
cassis, a rich blackcurrant liqueur that's used to make
the classic French aperitif, Kir. Put the blackberries, gin,
cassis, and ice cubes in a blender or food processor and
whizz until the fruit is puréed. Press the mixture through
a sieve to remove any pips. Mix in the apple juice, pour
into tumblers half-filled with crushed ice, and serve.

CHILLY [094] BLOODY MARY

This version of the classic "hair of the dog" cocktail is served ice cold and good 'n' spicy. For best results, use vodka straight from the freezer. Juice the tomatoes and red pepper and pour into a large jug. Stir in the vodka and add Worcestershire sauce, Tabasco, and salt and pepper to taste. Put the crushed ice in the jug before pouring into two tall glasses. Add the remaining ice cubes, stir, and pop in the celery sticks to serve.

8 vine-ripened TOMATOES
1 red PEPPER, deseeded and sliced
2 large measures iced VODKA
WORCESTERSHIRE sauce, to taste
TABASCO, to taste
SALT and PEPPER, to taste
8 ICE cubes, 4 crushed
2 short CELERY sticks, to decorate

[095]

RED DAWN

The pinker the flesh of a grapefruit the sweeter it will be, so using ruby grapefruits in this drink means that you get a pleasingly sweet tipple that retains the unmistakable tang of grapefruit. This cocktail couldn't be simpler to make. Use a citrus press or reamer to squeeze the juice from the grapefruits. Mix together the juice and the gin, pour into ice-filled tumblers, and serve.

2 ruby GRAPEFRUITS, halved
2 large measures GIN
ICE, to serve

200g/7oz frozen RASPBERRIES
1 measure TRIPLE SEC or Cointreau
2 measures TEQUILA
2 tsp caster SUGAR
freshly-squeezed LIME juice, to taste
100ml/3$^{1}/_{2}$ fl oz freshly-squeezed
ORANGE juice
ICE, to serve
2 LIME wedges, to decorate
maracas (optional)

[96]

ACAPULCO

Viva Mexico! Nothing beats an
ice cold Margarita and this super-
refreshing raspberry version won't
disappoint. Lime is an essential
ingredient whenever tequila is involved
and it works beautifully here with the sweet
raspberries. Blend together the raspberries,
Triple Sec or Cointreau, tequila and sugar.
Pour into a jug and stir in the lime and
orange juices. Add plenty of ice and
serve in Margarita glasses decorated
with wedges of lime on the rims.

1 medium PINEAPPLE, peeled
and chopped
2 ORANGES, halved
2 large measures dark RUM
2 measures COINTREAU or Grenadine
6 ICE cubes
sprigs of fresh MINT, to decorate

[097]
BEACH PARTY

You are on the beach, the sun is setting, the aroma of barbecued chicken fills the air … what's missing? A glass or two of this crowd-pleasing tropical rum punch, that's what! First, juice your pineapple. Next, use a citrus press or reamer to squeeze the juice from the oranges. Mix together the fruit juices and pour them, along with the rum and the Cointreau, into an ice-filled jug. Decorate with sprigs of mint.

Turn this into a sundae by leaving out the soda and adding some slices of fresh peach and a scoop of vanilla ice cream. Drizzle some extra strawberry liqueur over the top to finish and serve with long-handled spoons.

[098]
BOOZY STRAWBERRY SODA

300g/10^1/$_2$ oz STRAWBERRIES, hulled
2 measures strawberry LIQUEUR
2 large measures white RUM
2 large scoops good-quality STRAWBERRY ICE CREAM
chilled SODA water

A soda fountain for grown-ups, this is a dreamy blend of vitamin-C-packed strawberries, alcohol and – joy of joys – ice cream. It's got to be the ultimate summer treat! Blend the strawberries to a purée, then press them through a sieve to remove the seeds. Mix the purée with the liqueur and the rum, then pour into two sundae glasses. Add a scoop of ice cream to each, top up with soda water, and serve.

300g/10oz fresh CHERRIES, stoned OR
300g/10oz tinned cherries (drained weight)
2 measures VODKA
freshly-squeezed LIME juice, to taste
6 ICE cubes
caster SUGAR, to taste
2 twists of LIME zest, to decorate

[99]
CHERRY-OH!

Forget cherry pie, this is the only way to go ... . For a truly thrilling experience, try this sour-sweet concoction of delicious cherry and lime juices with vodka. Simply juice the cherries and then shake all the ingredients together in a cocktail shaker with ice. If the drink is too tart, add a sprinkle of sugar, and shake again. Pour into two martini glasses and serve decorated with twists of lime zest.

[100]
COMFORT
ZONE

Wrap yourself up in this creamy and indulgent cocktail, which is surely the next best thing to a cashmere blanket. Use a citrus press or reamer to squeeze the juice from the oranges. Pour the juice into a blender with the Grand Marnier, banana and ice cream. Blend until smooth and frothy and pour into two small wine glasses. Grate a little plain chocolate over the top of each glass to decorate, and serve.

2 ORANGES, halved
2 measures GRAND MARNIER
1 BANANA, peeled and cut into chunks
2 scoops VANILLA ICE CREAM
dark CHOCOLATE, to decorate

[INDEX]

Author's acknowledgments
I would like to thank the following suppliers for providing me with equipment to test my recipes: l'Equipe and Magimix for their juicers and KitchenAid for their blender.